Why I Love My
TEACHER

101 Dang Good Reasons

Ellen Patrick

ISBN 1-58173-400-X

Text design by Miles G. Parsons
Printed in Italy

1. You don't always believe me, but you believe in me.

2. You always forgive me—sooner or later.

—~—

3. You know how hard I try.

4. You know when I'm not trying hard enough.

—∞—

5. You're just plain nice.

6. When you're not nice, it's for a good reason.

7. You're patient.

—∿—

8. You're kind.

—∿—

9. You're smart.

10. You're on my side.

—⚬⚬⚬—

11. You're there every day.

12. Mom likes you.

13. I trust you.

14. You are pretty darn hard to fool.

15. You know everything.

16. You let us have fun.

—〜〜—

17. You like to have fun, too.

18. Sometimes I think you know just what it's like to be a kid.

—∞—

19. Don't tell anyone, but I think you are cool!

20. Sometimes I think you know what I am thinking.

21. I don't know how you do this, but you can see out of the back of your head.

22. You can hear everything.

23. You must be like some kind of superhero.

—ᴍ—

24. You make me believe in myself.

25. I am smarter than I was before I got in your class.

26. I still don't like homework, but at least you can get me to do it!

27. I wish every teacher was like you.

28. I wish every grown-up was like you.

—∞—

29. I even wish a lot of kids were like you!

30. I want to be like you when I grow up.

—⁓—

31. You let us goof off on the last day of class.

32. You always give me another chance.

33. You make me think about things.

—∿—

34. You make me laugh.

35. You taught me a lot of stuff I didn't even know I needed to know.

36. You teach me more than just book stuff.

—⁂—

37. I don't know how you get me to do the things you do.

38. When I don't know the answer, you help me find it.

—⚍—

39. When I do know the answer, you make me feel proud.

40. You teach me cool stuff.

41. You are pretty easy to talk to, for a grown-up.

42. You're nice to me even when I'm not nice to you.

43. You make our classroom feel like home.

44. You get it.

—ᵐᵐ—

45. I can understand what you tell me.

46. You always listen.

—⁂—

47. You are fair.

48. You are wise.

—◦◦◦—

49. You are strong.

50. You work hard (even a kid can see that).

—∿—

51. You do stuff you don't have to do.

52. I bet there's a lot you don't like doing, but you don't let on.

53. You know everything about me.

54. You don't talk down to us.

---

55. You make me feel important.

56. You don't let me get away with anything (much).

———

57. You're so great, you should be famous.

58. You're so great, you should be rich.

59. You should be on TV or in the newspaper.

60. You really listen to me.

—∿—

61. Everyone should have you as a teacher.

62. You wave to me when I see you in the grocery store.

63. You must like being a teacher, and that's lucky for me.

64. You're really good at talking to Mom.

—〜〜—

65. There's nobody else like you.

66. You put up with a lot.

—◈—

67. You never mind explaining—again.

68. Sometimes I actually want to do my homework.

69. Mom says you are all things to all people.

70. Mom says that if they gave out prizes for keeping a level head, you'd be covered up.

71. Mom says it isn't easy being you (but it looks easy).

—◦◦◦—

72. Mom says you have E.S.P.

73. Mom says you will get your reward in heaven, but I hope you get it before that.

74. Sometimes I don't get what Mom says, so it is a good thing that you do.

75. You know when we all need a piece of candy.

76. When I am sad, you cheer me up.

77. When I am worried, you tell me it is okay.

78. When I am happy, you are happy, too.

79. I know I can always count on you.

—∿∿—

80. You're brave.

81. You're friendly.

—◊◊◊—

82. You're funny.

83. You're tough.

—⧸⧸⧸—

84. You're totally amazing.

85. You get along with everyone.

86. Everyone likes you.

—〰—

87. You stick up for me.

88. You're understanding.

—◦◦◦—

89. You're good at everything.

90. You have a nice smile.

91. You have a good frown (it makes us behave)!

92. When you get mad, you don't stay mad.

93. You miss me if I am out sick.

—⁓—

94. You always tell the truth.

95. You tell good stories.

—⟋⟍—

96. You read good books to us.

97. You let us eat cookies (sometimes).

---∾---

98. Mom says you are one in a million.

99. All I know is, you are the greatest teacher ever!

100. I might not always show it, but I really appreciate you.

101. Of all the teachers in the world, I'm glad I got you.